WONDER WOMEN

Inspiring stories
of courage and
adventure

Greg Lewis

MAGIC RAT
BOOKS

TO DEMAND THE VOTE.

OFFICIAL PROGRAMME

OF THE

WOMEN'S CORONATION PROCESSION,

(Organized by the Women's Social & Political Union, 4, Clements Inn, W.C.)

SATURDAY, JUNE 17TH, 1911.

MRS. PANKHURST, Founder of the Movement & Hon. Sec. of the W.S.P.U.

Published by E. MARKS & SON, 35, Rosoman Street, Clerkenwell, E.C.

DOSSIER NAME:

WONDER WOMEN

VOTES FOR WOMEN

£1.40

WELSH SUFFRAGETTES, CORONATION PROCESSION, 1911

INTRODUCTION

The five stories in this book feature women with very different lives. They faced different challenges and chased different dreams.

But all have one thing in common: dedication. These women battled hard to achieve what they set out to do.

They worked not only to have their talents recognised, but to overcome barriers that they faced just because they were women.

Annie's story is one of courage and care in war.

The suffragettes risked all to ensure that women had the same democratic rights as men.

Amelia flew the Atlantic and became world famous.

Tracy came back from so many difficulties to win fame by tackling the world's seas.

Although Tanni cannot walk, she became one of the most famous and successful Welsh athletes of all time.

These are stories of adventure, danger, bravery, and skill – and each finds its own way to inspire us all.

TRICKY WORDS:

Democratic rights – Rights in a system where politicians are elected.

Racial prejudice – Intolerance or hatred against a person because of their race

15° West 10° 5° 0° Long. 5° East 10° 15°

FAROE IS.

NORWAY SWEDEN

Skagerrack

TH DENMARK

SEA

Terschelling L.S.

I C

IRELAND

WALES ENGLAND

London

HOL

GERMANY

BEL

Falmouth
SCILLY IS.
lish Channel

SWITZER-LAND

FRANCE

ITALY

y of

PORTUGAL

NEAN

e Port
an

500

BUFFALO, N.Y.

RÉPUBLIQUE FRANÇAISE

MINISTÈRE DE LA GUERRE

SOUS-SECRÉTARIAT D'ÉTAT
DU SERVICE DE SANTÉ MILITAIRE

CORPS des INFIRMIÈRES TEMPORAIRES
DES HOPITAUX MILITAIRES
(au titre étranger).

CARTE D'IDENTITÉ

Nom *Miss Brewer*
Prénoms *Annie Elizabeth*
Nationalité *anglaise*
Infirmière *major*
Domicile *New Port mon Conze*

Signature de la Titulaire

Annie Elizabeth Brewer

CACHET OFFICIEL
POUR AUTHENTIFICATION

FILE ONE:

A WELSH NURSE AT WAR
ANNIE BREWER

The First World War (1914-1918) was a hell on earth for millions of soldiers.

Much of the fighting took place on the battlefields of northern France where the British and French armies were dug into deep trenches, facing the German army in its own line of trenches a few hundred metres away.

These trench lines ran from the coast at the English Channel to the Swiss border, and became known as the Western Front.

Men were wounded and killed in their thousands and hundreds of thousands.

History books tell us much about the men who served. But women also played a prominent part, many of them as nurses on the front line. Behind the front an extensive system of casualty clearing stations and field hospitals had to be developed.

Nurses worked in terrible conditions, with shells raining down on them. Many died. But others cheated death and became heroes for the courage they showed.

Their stories are often as remarkable as those of the soldiers they helped save.

These women were the warriors of the hospitals – the angels of the battlefield.

TRICKY WORDS:

Extensive – Widespread, large.

Imagine you are working in one of these hospitals. There are so many casualties coming in it is hard to keep up. Sometimes you are working day and night to comfort and treat people. You are exhausted.

And you are working so close to the frontline that shells are landing close by. Explosions rock the tents and buildings in which you work. At any moment you too could be hit, but still you continue to treat and care for the young soldiers brought before you.

This was the life of Annie Brewer, a nurse from Newport, Gwent: a nurse whose story is so remarkable that she won more medals than most of the soldiers on the front.

★ ★ ★

Annie Brewer was born in November 1874 and grew up reading the popular stories about Florence Nightingale and the service she gave as a nurse in the Crimean War.

Annie decided she, too, wanted to be a nurse. By the age of 24 she was fully qualified and went to work in hospitals in England.

From the beginning she was never afraid of the most difficult and dangerous situations. In London, she worked in a special hospital set up to deal with frequent outbreaks of highly-infectious diseases such as smallpox, typhoid and diphtheria.

International holidays were not common in the early days of the twentieth century but Annie was a keen traveller. She visited Switzerland, Italy and Malta.

But France was her favourite country. She learned the language and developed a deep love for the nation.

Many of her journeys were taken with an elderly lady from Pontypridd. It was customary for wealthy people to employ a companion or nurse for long trips, and Annie looked after the lady while they travelled.

They were visiting Paris in August 1914 when the First World War – then referred to as the Great War – broke out.

Annie immediately said she wanted to help Britain and France, who were fighting together against Germany. The old lady travelled home alone and Annie joined a nursing organisation supported by the Red Cross.

Within weeks she was working in special hospitals near the front line.

The German army invaded France at the outbreak of the war and headed for the capital, Paris. The French army stopped them that September at the ferocious Battle of the Marne.

Annie was there, working with French nurses and tending the wounded French soldiers. They quickly got used to the Welsh nurse who spoke French well, but with an accent, and who was always full of kindness and care.

TRICKY WORDS:

Ferocious – Fierce and cruel.
Artillery shells – Explosives fired from large guns.

The Battle of the Marne marked the start of a long war for Annie.

The armies were no longer advancing or retreating. The soldiers dug trenches and faced each other across muddy battlefields. Each side bombarded the other with artillery shells. Soldiers lived in fear of being caught in one of these massive explosions and, as Annie moved nearer the front, it worried her, too.

But nothing stopped her from doing her work – even when she took part in one of the longest battles of the war and faced death herself.

★ ★ ★

The Battle of Verdun started in February 1916 and was to last for over 10 months. In that time there would be about 750,000 French and German casualties, with more than half being on the French side.

What made Verdun especially dreadful was the fact that so many thousands of artillery shells were fired on soldiers in such a small area – a narrow front line of only about 15 miles. One French officer said the battle proved that humanity was "mad".

Annie Brewer was at the centre of this horrible battle.

By this time she had risen to the rank of Commandant Major, which meant she was in charge of a large army hospital.

In a letter home to her mother she said the hospital she ran had 2,900 beds. 'My hair stands on end at the responsibility,' she wrote. She also told her mother that after one attack at Verdun she and her staff had carried out '229 operations in seven days' – more than 30 a day. She said that she and her staff were exhausted.

The need for supplies to treat so many casualties meant that in their letters home to friends and family nurses often asked for medical provisions and comforts for the soldiers.

Another hospital which Annie ran was in a chateau, a grand

country house four miles south of the town of Verdun. Before the war the beautiful house on the river Meuse was a haven of peace. In 1916, it was very different.

An American volunteer, who was working as an ambulance driver, remembered the scene: 'The chateau reeked with ether and iodoform,' he said, referring to two chemicals which were used as anaesthetics to put patients to sleep before an operation. 'Ambulance after ambulance came from the lines.'

★　★　★

Annie was able to photograph much of what she saw. There were no mobile phones, of course, and until shortly before the war professional photographers took the majority of photographs. People would go to a photographer's studio – a special room to have their picture taken.

But before Annie went to France a company called Eastman Kodak had developed what it called its Vest Pocket camera, a small black camera which could fit into a pocket or a small bag. These were as revolutionary as the mobile phone would be nearly a century later. For the first time people could buy a camera, which they could carry around and use, for quite a cheap price. During the war the company marketed it as 'the Soldier's Camera' and it sold in huge numbers.

Annie Brewer bought one and took it to war with her. She took photos of the trenches, of her colleagues, and of wounded soldiers being treated. She even took pictures of her and her friends having a laugh or joke. Experts say Annie's collection of photos is one of the finest set of pictures from the hospitals of the First World War.

★ ★ ★

Another large hospital Annie helped run had been created out of dozens of tents in farmland at Dugny-sur-Meuse, a village south of Verdun.

Dugny is a small village in beautiful countryside. Its full name shows that it is on the river Meuse.

Annie's hospital tents were arranged in rows behind a large house in the village. She was very busy there, dealing with hundreds of wounded from the front which was just a few miles away.

On August 18, 1917, the hospital came under heavy shellfire. Undaunted, Annie continued to work until a shell landed where she was working. Three of her nursing friends were killed instantly and many were injured, including Annie. A piece of hot metal from the exploding shell went into her leg and she also received a head injury which affected her sight. She later had to have an operation on her eyes.

For her courage that day she received the *Croix de Guerre* (Cross of War), one of the highest awards given by the French government for heroism in battle. On presenting it to her, a French general described Annie as 'a remarkable nurse' with a strength of 'morale and devotion' that had been 'clearly demonstrated time and time again'.

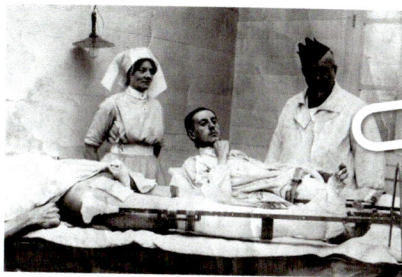

The general said that even under shellfire Annie had 'set the finest example of coolness and total disregard of danger, lavishing her attention on the wounded under fire from the enemy artillery'.

Annie was in a hospital bed with her head bandaged up when the medal was pinned onto her chest.

Annie's friends who died that day are remembered in a stained glass window in the Ossuary at Douaumont, the final resting place for the bones of 130,000 French and German soldiers who died in the battle.

The French remember Verdun as the worst battle of the war. It is said that the area around the town is the most shelled piece of land in the world. Today, on a hill overlooking the town, stands a statue commemorating the thousands killed in the battle that raged here for almost a year.

TRICKY WORDS:

Morale – Confidence and optimism.

The destruction in this area was so complete that a number of local communities were destroyed all together. The names of these places still exist and people are symbolically elected as the village mayor, but the land on which they stood was made uninhabitable by shelling. These are now villages in which no one lives.

They are known as 'the villages that died for France'.

★ ★ ★

Annie Brewer returned to the front after being wounded but she had not fully recovered her good health.

In April 1918, she collapsed and spent the next five months recuperating at a hospital in Monaco.

But she could not stay away for long. She wanted to get back to help. She returned to nursing, remaining in France after the war ended in November 1918 to help the thousands left injured and traumatised.

Then, when Annie learnt that her mother was ill, she returned to Wales to nurse her. Back in Newport, Annie became unwell again. She was exhausted and still in pain.

Annie's mother recovered but Annie suffered kidney failure and died on January 30, 1921, within a few weeks of her return to Wales. She was 46.

The brave nurse who had come through the horror of war, the hell of Verdun, succumbed to ill-health in bed at home.

A horse-drawn carriage carried her coffin to St Woolos cemetery in Newport. Over the years the location of the grave was lost. There was no headstone – but in 2014, a century on from the beginning of the First World War, her relatives located the grave and erected a headstone which befitted a hero.

During the war, the French Government had honoured Annie with a number of medals, including the *Croix de Guerre* she had earned at Dugny and the coveted *Médaille d'Honneur* (Medal of Honour), which she received for 'constant devotion shown to our wounded soldiers'. The British awarded her the *Mons Star*, the *War Medal* and the *Victory Medal* for her service.

After she died her family received a further medal from the office of the French president. The *Médaille de la Reconnaissance Français* – the Medal of French Gratitude – had been specially created for civilians who had volunteered to help the wounded and refugees of the war.

This collection of medals recognised Annie as one of the most highly-decorated women of the First World War and makes her a fitting symbol of the courage, dedication and care shown by nurses during that terrible conflict.

NEWPORT NURSE'S BURIAL.
Remarkable War Career.

The funeral took place at Newport yesterday of Nurse Annie Elizabeth Brewer, daughter of Mr and Mrs Brewer, of West-street, Newport. Nurse Brewer, who was generally well spoken of, had had a remarkable career. She was in France with a Cardiff lady when war broke out, and immediately joined the Anglo-French Nursing Expedition and was behind the lines at the first battle of the Marne. With Nurse A. E. Brewer occasional ... she remained in France, and after ... ceased accompanied the Army of Occupation. She returned home two weeks ago. ... nurse her mother, was taken ill and did not r...

She was for some time on the Somme and later at Verdun. She invariably accompanied the troops up the line and had been wounded in the head and struck with a piece of shrapnel in the leg. One of the hospitals where Miss Brewer was in charge was blown up by the Germans, and although a large number was killed she escaped uninjured. She had received several decorations from the French and British Governments, including the French Legion of Honour, Medaille de la Reconnaissance Francaise. Citation a l'Ordre de l'Armee Medaille D'Honneur, Croix de Guerre, with palm, the Mons Star, and the British War and Victory Medals. She was a fluent French speaker. Much sympathy is felt with her parents, who are much esteemed at Newport.

TRICKY WORDS:

Uninhabitable – Unsuitable for living in.

Recuperating – Recovery from illness.

Traumatised – Affected by emotional shock.

Succumbed to – Gave in to.

WONDER WOMEN DETECTIVE:

1. Can you name the two major battles in which Annie Brewer worked as a nurse?

2. Name at least three medals Annie was awarded.

3. What do you think Annie meant when she said, 'My hair stands on end at the responsibility'?

Answers on page 62

THINK ABOUT:

The most famous nurse in history is Florence Nightingale. She was known as 'The Lady with the Lamp', as paintings showed her nursing soldiers by lamplight. What nickname would you give to Annie?

FILE TWO:
THE SUFFRAGETTES

While Annie was risking her life to save soldiers on the Western Front, as a woman she was still classed as a 'second class citizen' in the UK.

In Britain at the time, women were not allowed to vote in elections and therefore had no say in who ran the government or who represented them as their Member of Parliament (MP).

Campaigns had been building for many years to ensure that women finally got the vote.

The leading voices belonged to a remarkable group of women who became known as the suffragettes.

WELSH SUFFRAGETTES, CORONATION PROCESSION, 1911

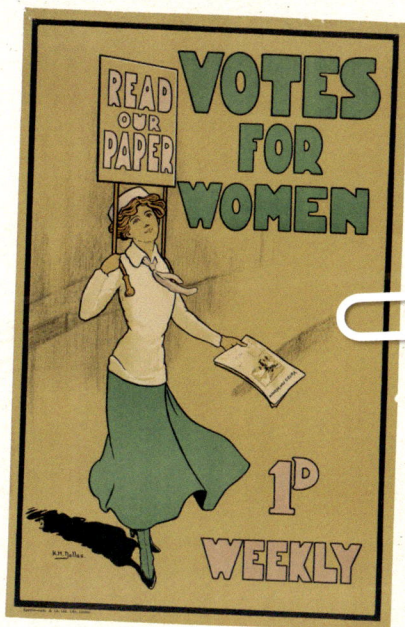

READ OUR PAPER
VOTES FOR WOMEN
1D WEEKLY

Although the Parliament at Westminster has existed for centuries, for most of its history only a very small number of wealthy, land-owning men had been allowed to vote or stand as MPs.

In the early 1800s there was some improvement, when suffrage – the right to vote – was extended to include more men, although these were still largely wealthy men.

The poor and all women were still not allowed to vote, so large campaigns developed and the law continued to change slowly.

At the end of the nineteenth century, many groups which campaigned for women to get the right to vote, came together. Some (called 'suffragists') believed in non-violent campaigning, but many women felt that more direct action needed to be taken.

One of those was Emmeline Pankhurst. She said that women had been campaigning politely for generations without getting anywhere, and that now they needed to get noticed.

She formed the Women's Social and Political Union with her three daughters in 1903. It was Emmeline's group of campaigners – who marched and held rallies – who became known as the 'suffragettes'.

They felt that enough was enough. There had been enough talking; something had to be done.

They put the issue of the women's vote on the political agenda, shocking the UK Government with some of their actions. They chained themselves to the railings of government buildings, smashed windows and even planted bombs.

At least one of them died for the cause. Emily Davison stepped in front of a horse owned by the king in 1913 as it was running in a famous race. She was knocked over and died later.

Emmeline Pankhurst's campaign had many supporters in Wales. Chief among them was Margaret Haig Thomas (later Margaret Mackworth through marriage).

Margaret was wealthy and privileged. She was very close to her father, David Thomas, who owned many businesses, including coalmines, and was a leading politician.

She studied history for a short time at Oxford University but came back to Cardiff to work for her father in an office.

She had been a very shy child and teenager but her passion for the rights of women was to bring her out of her shell.

In 1908, at the age of 25, she joined the Newport, Gwent, branch of Emmeline Pankhurst's organisation. She was soon hosting sometimes angry meetings across south Wales, and speaking passionately at them.

She also became a personal supporter of Emmeline's, joining her on some of her most daring exploits.

Margaret was not afraid to risk injury or jail in order to raise the profile of the suffragettes by getting their struggle into the newspapers.

Emmeline Pankhurst

Margaret Haig Thomas

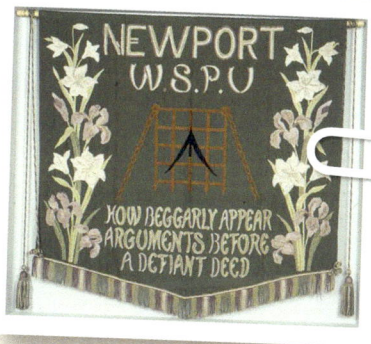

During the General Election campaign of 1910, Margaret jumped onto the side of a car which was carrying Herbert Asquith, the then prime minister.

In June 1913, she tried to blow up a post box with a homemade bomb. She was arrested but refused to pay a £10 fine which was imposed by

David Lloyd George

a court. She was sent to Usk jail, but went on hunger strike for five days, gaining even more attention for the cause. She was then released. Margaret received a special medal from Emmeline for her prison protest.

During the First World War Emmeline's organization decided to reduce its direct action so as not to disrupt the country at a time of war.

Margaret travelled with her father to the United States of America as representatives of the prime minister, David Lloyd George (who had sometimes been a target for the suffragettes).

On the way back the passenger boat on which they were travelling – the *Lusitania* – was struck by a torpedo from a German U-boat.

While her father made it to a lifeboat, Margaret had to jump into the sea. She clung to a piece of wood until she was rescued by a fishing boat.

Margaret was lucky: 1,201 people died – including three stowaways, whose names are not known.

She decided that surviving such a terrible event was a sign that she should continue to fight even harder for the causes she believed in.

Her father had been given a place in the House of Lords, one of the chambers of the British Parliament, for his services to the wartime government. He had been given the title 1st Viscount Rhondda.

When he died in 1918, Margaret inherited this title from him: she was to be known as 2nd Viscountess Rhondda.

This entitled her to sit in the House of Lords, but there was a problem: according to the law, women were not allowed in the House of Lords!

Margaret thought this was ridiculous and unfair. She took legal action and had the rule overturned.

But a leading member of the government, who opposed women having rights, such as the right to vote, fought back and she was still unable to take her seat in the House of Lords.

She continued to fight for the rest of her life for the rights of women to sit in the Lords, but the first woman did not take her place there until a few weeks after Margaret died in 1958.

However, the suffragettes achieved success long before then. In 1918 a law was passed which allowed all women over 30 to vote. All men over 21 were also allowed to vote.

Around the same time another law allowed women to stand for Parliament. The first woman MP was elected in December 1918, just after the fighting of the First World War ended.

That was also the first General Election in which women voted.

It was not until 1928 that the voting age for women was lowered to 21, making female voters equal to male ones.

That same year Emmeline Pankhurst died. Margaret helped organize a memorial and statue to her.

TRICKY WORDS:

U-Boat – A German submarine.

Stowaways – People hiding on a ship without the crew knowing.

Margaret spent many years at the head of the businesses she had inherited from her father. It was unusual for a woman to be a director of a company at the time and she became the first-ever woman president of the business organization, the Institute of Directors.

She started a magazine which was to publish many famous writers, including George Orwell and Virginia Woolf.

And she also set up her own organization to continue to fight for women's rights and the rights of children.

★ ★ ★

Elizabeth Andrews

Margaret was not the only Welsh woman inspired by Emmeline Pankhurst.

Elizabeth Andrews came from a very different background to the wealthy Margaret, but she fought the same fight.

One of 11 children, she had to leave school at the age of 12 to support her mother at home. Her father and brothers were miners.

Elizabeth was a vocal campaigner and, by the time women were given the vote in 1918, she was already an experienced public speaker.

She then became one of the woman organizers of the Labour Party, and campaigned for cleaner and safer conditions in the coalmines. Her father and two of her brothers had died from lung diseases brought on from the coal dust in the mines.

In her writing, Elizabeth described how important it was that people remembered votes for women had been a hard-won freedom which had many wider effects on society.

'The Vote broke down age-long barriers to women in all the professions,' she wrote in her book *A Woman's Work Is Never Done*. 'It opened the door for women to enter Parliament, local and national councils, law, medicine, industry, religion and all social work. Old customs were overthrown. No longer could the men persuade us that women were their intellectual inferiors.'

She also campaigned for better lives for the children of the South Wales Valleys and was one of the people who helped create the first nursery school in Wales. It opened in Ynyscynon in the Rhondda in September 1935.

★ ★ ★

Megan Lloyd George was the first Welsh woman to be elected an MP for Wales. Her father, David Lloyd George, had been Chancellor of the Exchequer and then Prime Minister, meaning that Megan had grown up in No. 11 Downing Street, then No. 10.

She learned all about the life of a politician and even travelled to France with her father when he signed the peace treaty at Versailles at the end of the First World War.

She was outspoken and a great public speaker, and made women's rights a big part of her campaigning.

In 1929, she was elected to represent Anglesey in the House of Commons. She represented the Liberal Party between 1929 and 1951, but switched to the Labour Party and represented the people of Carmarthen between 1957 and 1966.

She was one of the founders of 'Parliament for Wales', a campaign which would eventually lead to devolution and the creation of the Welsh Government and Senedd.

She also led efforts to resist the flooding of the village of Capel Celyn, in the Tryweryn Valley, near Bala, to create a reservoir for water for industry in Liverpool. She and campaigners could not stop the plan, though, and, in 1965, 70 villagers were forced to leave their homes and the village was flooded.

The destruction of the village is still a matter of huge controversy today, with many 'Cofiwch Dryweryn' ('Remember Tryweryn') murals having been painted around Wales as unofficial memorials. In 2005, the then leaders of Liverpool City Council apologized for the hurt caused by the decision to flood the village.

Did You Know?

The voting age in UK General Elections is now 18. People aged 16 and 17 can vote in Wales in elections for Senedd Cymru, the Welsh Parliament.

TRICKY WORDS:

Devolution – The transfer of powers from the UK Government to the nations of the UK, such as the Welsh Government.

WONDER WOMEN DETECTIVE:

1. What were the suffragettes campaigning for?

2. How did Margaret Haig Thomas help get attention for the suffragette movement?

3. Name two other Welsh women who helped gain more equality for women.

Answers on page 62

THINK ABOUT:

Do people today still think that girls and women are weaker and less intelligent than boys and men?

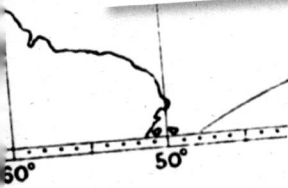

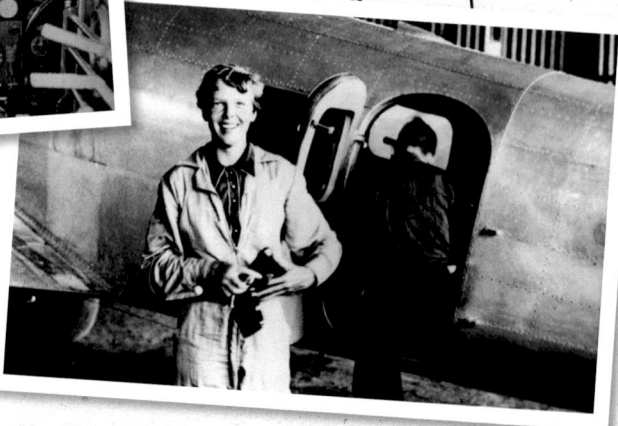

60°

50°

40°

30·1

30·2 | & over

HIGH

Tropi

60°   50°

0

FILE THREE:

WHEN FRIENDSHIP CAME TO BURRY PORT

AMELIA EARHART

In the summer of 1928 a seaplane touched down on a calm stretch of water off the Welsh coast.

It was lunchtime on a sunny Monday afternoon when people in Burry Port heard the aircraft circle the town before coming into land.

A seaplane is fitted with special floats, instead of wheels, so that it can land, taxi, and 'park' on the water.

This one, which was called *Friendship*, pulled up close to a buoy and one of its crew tied it up by rope.

A fisherman rowed out to the plane and found that it had three people on board: two men named Wilmer Stultz and Louis Gordon, and a 29-year-old woman named Amelia Earhart.

Friendship had taken off just under 21 hours earlier on June 17 from the coastal town of Trepassey in Newfoundland, Canada. And on this historic flight, Amelia became the first woman in the world to cross the Atlantic by air.

The three of them had flown through rain, mist, and fog so dense that for much of the flight they could see virtually nothing in front of them.

And it was because of the bad weather that *Friendship* had landed in Wales – and not Southampton in England, where dignitaries and journalists from all over the world were waiting for them.

With fog filling the sky, they had come down low when they were approaching Ireland. As they scanned the horizon, Amelia spotted a cruise ship and handwrote a note asking where they were. She put the note in a paper bag and weighted it with an orange.

The aircraft then flew low over the cruise ship and Amelia dropped the bag onto the ship's deck.

The aircraft circled the ship while the ship's crew wrote a message which could be seen from the air. It told them that they were 75 miles east of the Irish port of Queenstown, which is now known as Cobh.

Amelia and the two men had used up precious fuel in waiting for the message from the ship, so when they spotted the next coastline they decided to land.

The man who had rowed out to them was a well-known local character who had been shocked to see an aircraft landing on the water.

When Amelia opened the door, she shouted to him: 'Where are we?'

She was told she had landed in Wales.

Amelia and the other two were surprised but relieved. They might not have reached their destination yet, but they were safe and Amelia had made history.

Did You Know?

While the name of the town of Trepassey is most likely from the French language, some believe that the 'Tre' part might come from the Welsh for town. It could be true, because a Welshman named Sir William Vaughan, from Carmarthenshire, tried to establish a Welsh colony in Newfoundland in the seventeenth century, including the area around Trepassey, although most of the Welsh settlers later left.

The seaplane was towed into Burry Port harbour and cheering crowds came out to welcome Amelia.

As she climbed up the harbour steps, Amelia was surrounded by people who wanted to pat her on the back. A young boy actually pulled off her headscarf and ran off with it. He was never identified but perhaps the scarf is still tucked away somewhere in an attic in Burry Port.

While Amelia and her two companions were given tea in a local factory someone began to ring the newspapers to tell them about this historic event.

Amelia's flight of 2,200 miles was the biggest news story in the world and people everywhere had been waiting to hear if she was safe.

'I thoroughly enjoyed the trip,' Amelia told the *Western Mail* newspaper. 'I would do it again any time.'

The coast where Amelia landed, Burry Port Harbour and the Memorial unveiled by Sir Arthur Whitten Brown.

Amelia spent the night at the Ashburnham Hotel before returning to the harbour the next day to find the aircraft refuelled and ready to go.

Local schoolchildren were given the day off so that they could come down to see Amelia board the aircraft again. Large crowds watched as the aircraft taxied on the sea and took off into the sky.

'The harbour sides were thickly lined with people, who gave a rousing cheer as Miss Earhart and her flying companions left,' wrote the *Daily Express*.

Sadly, Amelia had gone before being able to have an historic meeting.

Sir Arthur Whitten Brown, who, with his partner Sir John Brown, had made the first successful non-stop crossing of the Atlantic Ocean in 1919, lived in Sketty, Swansea, and had heard about Amelia's arrival.

He rushed to Burry Port that morning, eager to shake her hand and offer her a large bouquet of flowers to celebrate her achievement.

But he arrived too late and was being rowed across Burry Port docks as the aircraft took off. Sir Arthur never got to meet Amelia.

It was a shame as at the time crossing the Atlantic by air was extremely dangerous. In the years between Brown's crossing and that historic flight by Amelia many people died trying to fly across the ocean.

Brown later unveiled a memorial to Amelia's flight in Burry Port.

★   ★   ★

While it was amazing to be the first woman to cross the Atlantic by air, Amelia wanted more.

She was disappointed that she did not get to be the pilot. She said she felt carried like 'a sack of potatoes'.

Amelia loved to fly. She had trained as a nurse but, when she was about 21, she had visited Toronto in Canada and seen an aerial display by a First World War flying ace. She was fascinated by the way that the aircraft dived and flew over the crowd.

In December 1920, she had been in Long Beach, California, with her father when they had met a pilot named Frank Hawks.

He had offered to take Amelia up in his aircraft. By the time the aircraft had risen into the sky Amelia knew that flying was her future.

She immediately decided to take flying lessons, but they were expensive. She worked in all sorts of jobs to raise the money. She eventually saved up enough to buy a small two-seater biplane which she nicknamed *The Canary* because it was painted yellow.

In 1922, she broke her first world record, flying to an altitude of 14,000 feet, the highest a female pilot had flown at the time. This record got her into the newspapers and led to her being on board the aircraft which crossed the Atlantic and landed in Burry Port in June 1928.

★   ★   ★

After becoming famous when she landed in Wales, Amelia was determined to make the flight across the Atlantic again. But this time she would be the pilot and there would be nobody else with her.

She trained hard, learning how to cope alone in the sky and how to navigate from place to place, making sure she got to where she wanted to be. This was not easy in these early years of flying as there wasn't as much equipment as there is today.

On May 20, 1932, four years after she landed in Wales, she set out to fly the Atlantic again – but this time on her own.

She left Newfoundland in a single-engine aircraft which she called *The Little Red Bus*. Hundreds of people gathered to watch her take-off that evening and then turn east on the long flight through darkness and across nothing but open sea.

It was freezing cold in the aircraft at 12,000 feet. It was dark all around, except for a silvery full moon, whose light glinted on small icebergs in the sea far below.

She passed through a thunderstorm which damaged the altimeter – the instrument which told her how high she was flying – and caused the aircraft's exhaust to start belching out smoke.

Then, as dawn began to break, she noticed that thick ice was building on the wings of the plane. She must have gained too much height and the air around the plane was freezing cold. Ice is heavy. It was likely to weigh down the plane or cause its controls to seize up. Amelia had to get rid of it – and quickly.

She pushed forward on the controls of the aircraft and the nose of the plane dipped. She was going into a dive, descending quickly to melt the ice on the wings and find warmer air.

Without the altimeter to tell her how quickly she was descending and how close she was to the sea, she had to keep alert in case she dived straight into the water.

She gritted her teeth and dived through the clouds, feeling the ice break off the wings as the plane plunged downwards.

As she emerged from the clouds and saw the sea ahead of her, she pulled back on the aeroplane's joystick and the plane levelled out.

She was now only a few hundred feet above the water, but the ice had melted. Ahead of her, the sun was rising in the east. She must be nearing Europe. But where was she? There were no landmarks to help her, only sea stretching out for miles all around.

Then she saw land. She wondered if it was Wales again or even France, where many famous aviators came from.

She turned towards it. As she neared the coast, a fishing boat fired a flare, which she took as a good omen – a welcome.

She found a railway line and followed it, knowing it would eventually lead to a town. The exhaust of the aircraft continued to belch out black smoke. To people down below it looked as if the aircraft was on fire. They prayed for the pilot.

TRICKY WORDS:

Descending – Going down.

Amelia could not find an airfield. With fuel low and the noises from the exhaust getting worse, she found the largest, flattest field she could, and landed.

It was 1.45 pm on May 21, 1932. She had been in the air for 14 hours and 56 minutes. Now she just had to find out where she was.

She saw a small cottage and walked over to it. An elderly couple answered the door.

'Where am I?' Amelia asked.

The couple looked at her. They were surprised and confused. Who was this woman with short but untidy hair and an exhausted face, and why didn't she know where she was!

'Ireland,' they said. 'You're in Ireland.'

Amelia smiled. She had made it! She was the first woman in history to fly solo across the Atlantic.

When she told the couple who she was they invited her in for a cup of tea.

They later drove her to the post office in the nearest city, Derry, where she was able to report to the newspapers that she had arrived safely and achieved the record.

Later, having been asked about the danger of her journey, she spoke about its beauty. 'The stars seemed near enough to touch, and never before have I seen so many,' she said.

★ ★ ★

After the flight Amelia became friends with Eleanor Roosevelt, the wife of the president of the United States, and together they promoted many issues trying to make life better for American women.

Amelia went on to be the first woman to fly across the Pacific Ocean and continued to want to break records.

In 1937, with a navigator called Fred Noonan, she attempted to make the first-ever flight around the world.

They had made it three-quarters of the way when, while crossing the vast Pacific, they were unable to find Howland Island where they were to refuel, and the aircraft was lost somewhere at sea.

Amelia was always aware of the hazards involved in what she was trying to achieve but she felt compelled to face the challenges. She is remembered as one of the world's greatest pioneering aviators.

And Burry Port is proud of its part in her wonderful story.

Did You Know?

The site where Amelia Earhart landed in Wales is subject to a little local rivalry! As she landed in the sea, it has been difficult to mark the exact spot. Her aircraft was towed into Burry Port and there are two memorials there marking this as the place she landed. But there is also a memorial a short walk along the coast in the village of Pwll, from where some say her plane could be seen as it came into land. It is something locals continue to discuss!

FIRST WOMAN TO FLY THE ATLANTIC OCEAN
Y FENW GYNTAF I HEDFAN Y WERYDD

Trepassey *The George* Burry Port
Newfoundland Porth Tywyn
COMMEMORATIVE BOOKLET

amelia earhart
FIRST WOMAN TO FLY THE ATLANTIC
18 JUNE 1928

BURRY PORT's HISTORIC AVIATION EVENT
THE SEAPLANE "FRIENDSHIP"
in BURRY PORT HARBOUR
18th June, 1928
Price—£1.25

TRICKY WORDS:

Hazards – Dangers.

Compelled – Forced.

Pioneering – To be the first to do something.

WONDER WOMEN DETECTIVE:

1. What was the weather like when Friendship landed on the sea off the Welsh coast?

2. Why were children given a day off school?

3. What other records did Amelia set or try to break?

Answers on page 63

THINK ABOUT:

What do you think the children of Burry Port learned from witnessing Amelia make history?

What qualities do you think Amelia Earhart had which helped her in her adventures?

FILE FOUR:

TRACY SAILS THE WORLD

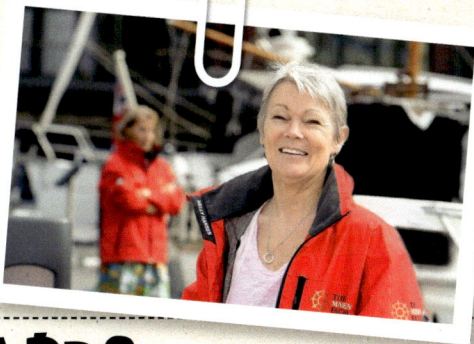

TRACY EDWARDS

A cheering crowd of 50,000 people lined the quayside. The noise was deafening as the yacht sailed closer, and the tired but elated faces of the crew came into view.

Everyone in the crowd chanted the same word over and over: '*Maiden! Maiden! Maiden!*'.

The yacht, called *Maiden*, was the first to circumnavigate – sail around – the world with an all-female crew.

She had come through a tornado with winds so strong they had damaged her mast and swirled the yacht around in the sea.

She had climbed stormy waves, the crew using every bit of their energy and skill to stay on course. And she had faced the curse of having no wind in her sails at all, becoming stuck on the ocean, losing time in the race.

But through the endeavour of her crew, *Maiden* had done what many people said she would not: she had finished one of the most difficult yachting races in the world.

TRICKY WORDS:

Tornado – A rapidly whirling column of air.
Endeavour – Great, and often brave, effort.

There had been doubters because sailing was a sport dominated by men. Many had scoffed at the idea that a yacht crewed only by women could achieve such a feat.

But *Maiden* had been the dream of someone who did not back down from a challenge.

And she smiled now as she saw the reception the yacht received. Her name was Tracy Edwards and this is her inspirational story.

Tracy was born in Reading, England, in 1962, but her upbringing focused very much on her Welsh roots, which were packed with the spirit of adventure.

Her father, Antony, was from a long line of train drivers, miners, and mariners. Her great-grandfather, who was from Merthyr Tydfil, had sailed on coal ships out of Newport and Swansea; her grandfather had been a fighter pilot in the First World War.

There was quite a bit of adventure in her parents, too.

Her father, Antony, was an electronics engineer and her mother, Patricia, a dancer, but they had met at a car rally in which they had both been driving.

Antony was also a keen yachtsman, and when Tracy was eight, he took her and her brother sailing to the Isle of Wight.

Remarkably, the girl who would become one of the most famous sailors in the world was very seasick on this first journey!

But there was to be much sadness in Tracy's childhood. Her father died suddenly and her mother, who had an illness called multiple sclerosis, began to get more and more unwell. Tracy went to a comprehensive school in Wales where she rebelled.

She lived with her mother, who had remarried and settled in a village called Llanmadoc on the Gower Peninsula.

At 16, Tracy went to work as a nanny in Greece and then found work on yachts being delivered around the world.

She spent five years as a crewmember, learning many of the skills that she would use during her career and crossing the Atlantic Ocean four times. This experience helped her gain a place in a crew for the prestigious Whitbread Round the World Yacht Race in 1985. Tracy was one of only five women among the 260 sailors taking part.

The race was run over different legs and took nine months to complete.

On reaching Cape Town in South Africa she changed boats and joined a previously all-man crew, which did very well.

It reached Auckland in New Zealand just seven minutes ahead of the next boat. This was the narrowest winning margin ever on any leg of the race.

But the race went on, and Tracy began to discuss her dream with the other crew members. Although she was in her early 20s she had already decided that what she wanted to do was to lead a crew made up only of women to compete in the race.

This was a big dream as, not only was the sport dominated by men, but many people in the sport felt men were needed on the yachts.

The first thing she had to do was go to the bosses of the race and ask if there were any rules against all-women crews. There were not.

But that was just the first hurdle she had to overcome.

Now, she had to raise £1.8 million to get a boat, crew and funds to train and race. She discussed the idea with many wealthy people whom she would need to sponsor a yacht.

TRICKY WORDS:

Mariners – Sailors.

Sponsor – An individual or company that supports a sports project, usually with money, and puts its name or logo on the sports kit – or, in this case, on a yacht.

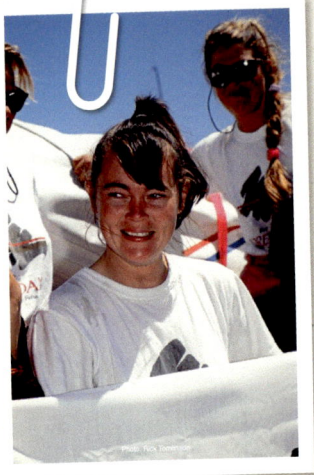

Most thought it would not happen. They did not think a crew made up only of women could complete the race, and would not give her money.

She had to mortgage her house and borrow money. In 1987, she bought a rundown yacht in South Africa and brought her back to England on a container ship. But the yacht was such a wreck she needed a complete refit.

By now, Tracy was heavily in debt and running out of options. She could not get any help from companies in Britain.

It was then that King Hussein of Jordan stepped in to help and Royal Jordanian Airlines became the yacht sponsor.

Tracy's 58-foot long yacht was finally made seaworthy and ready to race.

Tracy called her *Maiden*. This was a playful name. The word 'maiden' is an old-fashioned name for a young woman, but it also means something done for the first time. *Maiden* would be the first yacht to race around the world with an all-women crew.

Tracy tried out the yacht and her new crew of 12 in a special warm-up race, which started in Cadiz in Spain and crossed the Atlantic to Santa Domingo in the Dominican Republic.

Maiden came second, beating the winner of the previous Round the World race.

Things were looking very hopeful for the big race – the Whitbread Round the World Yacht Race of 1989–1990.

There were to be six legs in all.

The first leg covered almost 6,000 miles of the Atlantic Ocean, starting in Southampton on the south coast of England and finishing at Punta del Este in Uruguay.

The boats left Southampton on September 2, 1989.

But *Maiden* struggled. She reached Uruguay third in her class and now faced the hardest leg of the race: a journey of more than 7,000 miles east across the Southern Ocean to Fremantle in Australia.

This was a terrible journey, taking five hard weeks. All the yachts were battered by the weather and the seas.

One man from one of the boats was drowned, and seven people in total had to be saved after being swept overboard from different yachts.

One of Tracy's crew was among those who had to be rescued from the water.

But *Maiden* did very well. She won Division D in which they were competing. She was the first British boat to win anything in the Round the World race for 12 years.

Crowds stood in Fremantle harbour and cheered as it arrived.

But the journey had taken its toll on the boat and it took several days to fix the damage to the masts and rigging. As the female crew worked to fix *Maiden* they noticed that the onlookers, including fellow sailors and sailing journalists, had started to change their opinion about the all-women crew.

They had begun to believe that *Maiden* could actually complete the race, although many said she could not.

The third and next leg of the race was the shortest, although it was still more than 3,000 miles.

This went from Fremantle in Australia to Auckland in New Zealand. Again, *Maiden* came first in her division.

Tracy was starting to really make the news. She arrived in Auckland to learn she had been voted 'Yachtsman of the Year'. She was the first woman ever to win the award.

The fourth leg started on February 4, 1990. It was another long leg, with the yachts having to travel from Auckland back to Punta del Este in Uruguay – another stretch of more than 6,000 miles.

On this leg the women became the first all-female crew to round Cape Horn at the southern tip of South America.

But a lot went wrong.

They had bad luck with the weather, and the sea and wind caused damage to the yacht's generator and wheel. By the time she reached Uruguay, *Maiden* was in a terrible state and had been overtaken in her division of the race.

It seemed now that they would not catch up.

But they sailed on through the fifth leg to Fort Lauderdale in Florida, United States of America.

There, the crew arrived waving to the crowds, showing that they weren't downhearted by the bad luck they had suffered. Their good spirits further endeared Tracy and her crew to the crowds.

The sixth and last leg would bring them home across the Atlantic from the United States to Southampton.

On the 4,000-mile stretch *Maiden* was battered by a tornado and storms, but returned to an amazing welcome.

Hundreds of boats met her off the English coast and sailed into the harbour with her. Thousands of cheering people waited on the quayside.

Maiden had won two legs of the race and Tracy had become famous around the world. She had completely changed people's perceptions about women in ocean racing. She had shown that, given the same opportunities, female sailors could do everything that their male counterparts could do.

But Tracy's dream had come at a financial cost. She had to sell the yacht to pay debts.

Tracy went back to live on the Gower where she bought a small farm.

But her mind settled on a new challenge: to break the world record for the fastest non-stop circumnavigation of the world and win the Jules Verne Trophy. (Jules Verne was the writer of a famous book called *Around the World in 80 Days*.)

This was a massive challenge. The record at the time (71 days and 14 hours) was held by a Frenchman. It had taken him four years and seven attempts to get that record.

Tracy raised a huge amount of money and bought a 92-foot catamaran that she named after her main sponsor, a company called Royal and Sun Alliance.

In February 1998, the crew of 10 women – captained by Tracy – set sail from France and reached the equator in record time.

It was looking good, with the yacht often sailing more than 400 miles a day. Tracy had covered 15,200 miles when disaster struck.

In strong winds and heavy seas, a huge wave slammed into the catamaran from behind. In the darkness the crew struggled to keep their feet and control the boat. They were in great danger, and were very tired, as this was their 43rd gruelling day at sea.

Then there was a creaking and a crack, and the mast of the catamaran broke and crashed against the deck.

The catamaran was in the Atlantic, still 2,000 miles away from South America. The crew managed to repair the mast well enough to sail on towards safety in Chile. But the attempt on the record had to be abandoned. It was a huge disappointment for Tracy because she had been on course for success.

Tracy continued ocean racing, breaking other records, and she continued to be an inspiration for many. She started work to help children stay safe online and gave speeches about her life.

TRICKY WORDS:

Gruelling – Extremely tiring.
Psychology – The study of human behaviour.

Tracy had not had a happy time at school but she was determined to be a life-long learner. She went to university and passed a degree in psychology.

Through her charity *The Maiden Factor Foundation*, Tracy has committed a lot of her time to highlighting the plight of girls around the world who are not able or allowed to go to school.

In some countries only boys are permitted to study, or families are so poor they cannot send their children to school.

Tracy has set her heart on battling this injustice with the same dedication with which she set sail on many hazardous voyages to sea.

WONDER WOMEN DETECTIVE:

1. What was remarkable about Tracy's first journey out to sea as a child?

2. What was Tracy's 'big dream'?

3. How did Maiden and her crew change people's perceptions of what women were capable of?

Answers on page 64

THINK ABOUT:

What is your 'big dream' for the future?

FILE FIVE:

THE GIRL WHO WENT FOR GOLD

TANNI GREY-THOMPSON

Tanni Grey-Thompson's sporting and personal achievements would fill a large part of this book if we listed them all.

She has a cupboard filled with medals, is a campaigner for the rights of people with disabilities, and a member of the UK's House of Lords.

She was born with spina bifida, a condition affecting the spine, and has used a wheelchair since she was a child. But, throughout her childhood, she was determined to be treated the same as other children and to pursue her dream of becoming an athlete.

She was born in Cardiff in July 1969 and had an older sister, Sian, who was still only a toddler when Tanni was born.

It is because of Sian that Tanni is called 'Tanni'.

Her parents had actually called her Carys but Sian said the new baby was 'tiny' and, when she said it, it sounded like Tanni.

The name Tanni just stuck – and was to become world-famous.

It was through horse-riding that Tanni first experienced freedom. It was great being so high up in the saddle and above everyone else.

She began to see athletes using wheelchairs competing in sports on television and she thought she could do the same.

When she was 12 she represented Wales in the Junior National Games at Stoke Mandeville, a hospital in England where there is a well-known centre dealing with spinal injuries. She won a gold and a silver medal in the wheelchair races.

Throughout her teens she would continue to go to the Junior National Games, and get better and better.

She was so successful that she won a Junior Sports Personality of the Year Award in Wales, and then five medals at the British Paraplegic Games in 1987.

That same year she was chosen to represent Great Britain in her first international competition in Vienna.

She experienced the joy of being part of a major team and travelling to enjoy the sport. It was very exciting – and there was very much more to come.

All the while she trained very hard, using a track in Bridgend and, when the winter weather got too wet, a multi-storey car park. At the time there were few, if any, dedicated facilities for athletes using wheelchairs.

Tanni was a pioneer, determined to succeed and to improve life for fellow athletes. Plus she had a major goal: to compete in the Paralympics (the Olympic Games for athletes with disabilities), which were to be held in Seoul, South Korea, in 1988.

Tanni was determined to be there.

She continued to train hard, even as she studied for her A-levels and then went to Loughborough to start university.

To get to Seoul, Tanni needed to get noticed by the selectors – the people who decided which athletes would feature in the Great Britain team.

In April 1988, she won the 60-metre and 100-metre races at the National Disabled Student Games in record times.

She then represented Great Britain in a tournament in Dallas, Texas, against athletes from all over the United States and Canada. She set personal bests in the 100-metre, 200-metre, and 400-metre races.

When her first year at university ended and she came home to her family in Cardiff, she found a letter waiting for her.

She had done it. She had been picked to compete in the Paralympics!

That October, she flew to South Korea to be with the Great Britain team. Her luggage consisted not only of her clothes and her wheelchair but also spare wheels and tyres.

Tanni felt a lot of pressure. She had hoped to do really well in the 100 metres but she came fourth. Then she had a bad 200-metre race.

That meant only the 400-metre race remained.

She put everything into it and, in the final, she rushed home in third place, finishing in 81 seconds – a new British record!

That bronze medal in Seoul was the first of many top awards to come.

But almost immediately Tanni faced a setback. She had an infection in her back and had to go into hospital for an operation.

Back at university, where she was studying politics, Tanni tried her best to train whenever she had a spare moment. But she lost a year out of competition, unable to race on the track.

Then, in 1990, she was fit again. She won two silver medals and a bronze at the World Championships in the Netherlands and came third in the 800-metre race at a special event at the Commonwealth Games in Auckland, New Zealand, where she represented Wales.

By now, she had also become fascinated by road racing, an exciting but dangerous part of athletics. On some downhill stretches the racers can reach speeds of 40 or 50 miles an hour.

TRICKY WORDS:

Paraplegic – Someone who cannot move the lower half of their body.

Determined to succeed, Tanni would go out training, with her sister riding on a push bike. Together, they covered miles and miles on the roads every week, with Tanni trying to get used to racing on road surfaces as opposed to the relative smoothness of the track.

Tanni's fresh determination grew out of a new personal goal: she wanted to race in the London Marathon. A marathon is a race over a distance of 26 miles. The London course winds around streets in the city and passes well-known landmarks such as the Tower of London and Buckingham Palace.

Tanni's target was to complete the marathon in under three hours.

After about 21 miles, Tanni got a puncture in one of the tyres of her chair and two athletes stopped to help her change it.

She recovered and raced on. When she crossed the line, she had smashed her target, crossing the finish line in two hours, 49 minutes. She came fourth out of the women athletes.

The following year she won three golds and a silver at the World Wheelchair Games at Stoke Mandeville, and she graduated from university.

All her training now was geared towards a massive set of challenges in 1992. That year was to be a huge one for Tanni. She went back to the London Marathon and won, and then began a record-breaking run of results.

She broke the world record for the 200 metres in Australia but then broke the record again at a competition in Canada.

She also broke the world records for the 100-metre, 400-metre, and 800-metre races.

She took part in a demonstration event at the Olympic Games in Barcelona. Demonstration meant the event was not awarded a full medal. She achieved a new personal best time in the 800 metres there, finishing the race in one minute, 55 seconds.

Alongside the Olympic Games in Spain were the Paralympics. This tournament was to be huge for Tanni.

Sport Wales National Centre
Canolfan Genedlaethol Chwaraeon Cymru

It had been four years since the last Paralympic games – when Tanni had done so well in South Korea – and, during those four years, she had been dreaming of racing in Barcelona.

All her dreams were to come true.

She won gold medals in the 100 metres, 200 metres, 400 metres, and 800 metres races. Every one of her times in those races was a Paralympic record. The 100-metre race time was a new world record – once again she had beaten her own world record!

Honours now flooded in. A newspaper described her as the 'Sportswoman of the Year' and she won the BBC Wales/Western Mail Welsh Sports Personality of the Year (a title she won three times in total).

From there, the successes just kept coming, and her trophy cabinet grew fuller.

She continued to break world records – and she was to break a total of 30 over the length of her whole career.

She won the women's division of the London Marathon a further five times (six in total!). In the Paralympics of 1996, which were held in Atlanta, USA, she won gold in the 800 metres and three silver medals.

Then four years later, at the Sydney Paralympics, she again won four gold medals, as she had in Barcelona.

At her fourth and final Paralympics – the Athens games in 2004 – she won gold in the 100 metres and 400 metres.

Over her whole Paralympic career, she won a total of 11 golds, four silvers, and a bronze.

To this hatful of medals she could add five golds, four silvers, and three bronze from the World Championships.

In 2000, she came third in the BBC Sports Personality of the Year for the UK. The fact that no provision had been made in the ceremony for her to be able to come on stage in her wheelchair to collect the prize sparked a debate across the UK about disabled access to services, shops and other buildings.

★ ★ ★

In her autobiography, *Sieze the Day*, Tanni described the tension she felt before a race.

She said there would be nerves in her stomach and she would keep glancing at her watch. She would look into the crowd to find family and other friendly faces that she recognised – people who would inspire her.

At the end of the race her family would be grinning and patting her on the back, as the big screen flashed the words *WORLD RECORD!*

But, despite everything, she said she has never felt that she has raced a perfect race. That illustrates the sense of perfection that top athletes often feel.

But, to onlookers, her career seemed a perfect example to others.

Tanni had raised the profile of athletes using wheelchairs, and of Paralympic sport, and she had challenged the way society viewed disabled people.

When she retired from sport she joined a number of organisations and charities, helping to educate them about how they support people with disabilities.

In 2010, she was offered a place in the House of Lords, where she has contributed to debates about sport and disability rights.

Married to another former athlete, Ian Thompson, she is now known as Lady Tanni Grey-Thompson.

Although her first name came out of the word 'tiny', her contribution to sport has been immense.

She is without doubt one of Wales' most successful athletes of all time.

TRICKY WORDS:

Immense – Huge.

WONDER WOMEN DETECTIVE:

1. What condition was Tanni born with that meant she had to use a wheelchair since she was as a child?

2. What is her real name and how did she get the name 'Tanni'?

3. Why might road racing be described as 'exciting but dangerous'?

Answers on page 64

THINK ABOUT:

Can you think of the best adjectives to describe Tanni Grey-Thompson?

TIMELINES

ANNIE BREWER:

1874	Annie Brewer is born in Newport.
1899	Annie Brewer qualifies as a nurse.
August 1914	The First World War breaks out while Annie is in France. She volunteers to work as a battlefield nurse.
1916	Annie is a nurse at the Battle of Verdun.
August 1917	Annie treats wounded soldiers while under heavy shell fire. She is badly wounded in an explosion. She receives the *Croix de Guerre* for her courage.
November 1918	An armistice ends the First World War.
January 1921	Annie dies in Newport.
2014	Annie's relatives locate her unmarked grave and erect a headstone.

THE SUFFRAGETTES:

1903	Emmeline Pankhurst forms the Women's Social and Political Union to step up the campaign for women's right to vote.
1908	Margaret Haig Thomas joins the Newport branch of the organization and speaks at many meetings.
1910	Margaret jumps on the side of the prime minister's car as part of a protest.

1913	Protests continue. Emily Davison dies after jumping in front of the king's racehorse. Margaret is jailed for trying to blow up a letter box.
May 1915	Margaret is almost killed when a German submarine sinks the ocean liner, *Lusitania*. She clings to a piece of wood and is rescued by a fishing boat.
1918	Margaret's father dies and she inherits a seat in the House of Lords – but it does not admit women. The first women are allowed to vote but they must be over 30 years old.
1928	Women over 21 are allowed to vote – the same as men.
1929	Megan Lloyd George becomes the first Welsh woman MP.

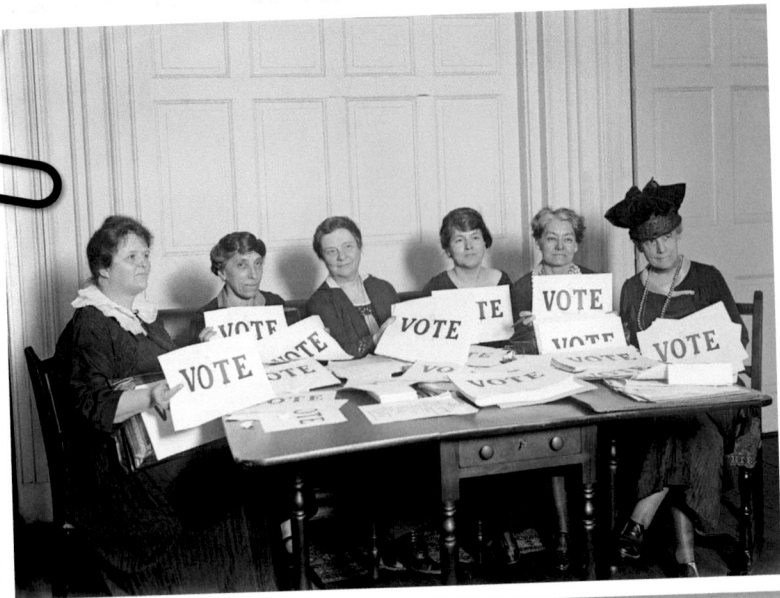

AMELIA EARHART:

1928	Amelia lands in the sea off Burry Port in an aircraft with two men. She is the first woman to cross the Atlantic by air – but she did not fly the plane.
1932	Amelia becomes the first woman to fly solo across the Atlantic, taking off in Canada and landing in Ireland.
1937	Amelia's plane is lost as she is attempting to fly around the world. It is assumed she ran out of fuel and crashed into the Pacific Ocean.

TRACY EDWARDS:

1985	Tracy joins a crew for the Round the World Yacht Race. She is one of only five women among the 260 sailors taking part.
1987	Tracy buys a rundown yacht. She has a dream to lead an all-women crew around the world.
1989	Tracy's boat *Maiden* starts in the Round the World Yacht Race with an all-women crew.
1990	*Maiden* returns to Britain after winning two legs of the race – a huge success. Tracy wins a number of awards.
1998	Tracy sets out to be the fastest to sail around the world but her boat is damaged by strong winds and heavy seas.

TANNI GREY-THOMPSON:

1969	Tanni Grey-Thompson is born in Cardiff.
1981	Tanni represents Wales at the Junior National Games.
1988	Tanni wins a medal at the Paralympic Games in Seoul, South Korea.
1992	Tanni wins the women's division of the London Wheelchair Marathon for the first time. She also wins four gold medals at the Paralympics in Barcelona, Spain.
1994	Tanni wins four gold medals at the World Athletics Championships in Berlin, Germany.
2000	Tanni wins four gold medals at the Paralympic Games in Sydney, Australia.
2002	Tanni wins the women's division of the London Wheelchair Marathon for a record sixth time.
2004	Tanni wins two gold medals at the Paralympic Games in Athens, Greece. She is voted BBC Wales Sports Personality of the Year for the third time.
2010	Tanni takes her seat in the House of Lords.

GLOSSARY

Altimeter – An instrument on a plane which shows the pilot how high it is flying.

Democracy – A system of government by elected representatives of the people.

Democratic rights – Rights in a system where politicians are elected.

Devolution – The transfer of powers from the UK Government to the nations of the UK, such as the Welsh Government.

Suffragettes – A name given to people who campaigned for women's suffrage (the right to vote).

U-Boat – A German submarine. It is a shortening of *Unterseeboot*, ie, under-sea boat.

Western Front – The areas of northern France and Belgium where much of the fighting during the First World War took place.

POEM

THREE VOICES AT BURRY PORT

'Look up! What's that?'
'A plane, I think.'
'But can planes float?
It's in the drink.'*

'It's landed now
Just off the shore.
Look! A woman
Opens the door.'

'Amelia,
From over the sea,
Bring her inside
For a cup of tea.'

'It's history
She's brought to town
By circling here
And coming down

At Burry Port.'
'She's done us proud!
Shout out "hooray!"
And shout it loud.'

'I've come so far
Through foggy sky,
But just some tea
Then I must fly.'

*in the sea

WONDER WOMEN DETECTIVE
ANSWERS

ONE: ANNIE, A WELSH NURSE AT WAR (from page 16)

1. Can you name the two major battles in which Annie Brewer worked as a nurse?
A. Annie was a nurse at the Battle of the Marne and the Battle of Verdun during the First World War.

2. Name at least three medals Annie was awarded?
A. Annie was awarded the *Croix de Guerre, Médaille d'Honneur* and the *Médaille de la Reconnaissance Français* from the French and the Mons Star, the War Medal and the Victory Medal from Britain.

3. What do you think Annie meant when she said, 'My hair stands on end at the responsibility'?
A. Annie said 'My hair stands on end at the responsibility' in a letter to her mother, in which she describes being in charge of a hospital with 2,900 beds. She meant that this was a huge responsibility which was, perhaps, daunting, frightening and almost shocking.

TWO: THE SUFFRAGETTES (from page 25)

1. What were the suffragettes campaigning for?
A. The suffragettes were campaigning for the rights of women to vote.

2. How did Margaret Haig Thomas help get attention for the suffragette movement?
A. As well as holding many meetings for the suffragettes, Margaret Haig Thomas also took part in acts which gained a lot of attention. In 1910, Margaret jumped onto the side of

a car which was carrying Herbert Asquith, the then prime minister. In June 1913, she tried to blow up a post box with a homemade bomb. She was arrested but refused to pay a £10 fine which was imposed by a court. She was sent to Usk jail but went on hunger strike for five days.

3. **Name two other Welsh women who helped gain more equality for women.**

A. Two other Welsh women who helped gain more equality for women were campaigner Elizabeth Andrews and politician Megan Lloyd George, who was the first Welsh woman to be elected an MP in Wales.

THREE: WHEN FRIENDSHIP CAME TO BURRY PORT (from page 36)

1. **What was the weather like when *Friendship* landed on the sea off the Welsh coast?**

A. When *Friendship* landed on the sea off the Welsh coast the weather was sunny.

2. **Why were children given a day off school?**

A. Children were given a day off school to watch Amelia Earhart and her two companions take off from Burry Port.

3. **What other records did Amelia set or try to break?**

A. Amelia set a number of records after becoming the first woman to cross the Atlantic by air. She became the first woman to fly solo across the Atlantic and the first woman to fly across the Pacific Ocean. She had also, when she was younger, broken the record for the highest altitude a woman pilot had reached. Amelia died in 1937 while attempting to make the first ever flight around the world.

FOUR: TRACY SAILS THE WORLD (from page 45)

1. **What was remarkable about Tracy's first journey out to sea as a child?**
A. Tracy's first journey out to sea as a child was remarkable because she was seasick. This was an unusual start for someone who was to become a great yachtswoman!

2. **What was Tracy's 'big dream'?**
A. Tracy's 'big dream' was to captain a boat crewed only by women in the Whitbread Round the World Yacht Race.

3. **How did *Maiden* and her crew change people's perceptions of what women were capable of?**
A. *Maiden* and her crew changed people's perceptions because many in the yacht-racing world had believed crews had to include men to be successful. Tracy's achievements showed that, given the same opportunities, women sailors could do everything that their man counterparts could do.

FIVE: THE GIRL WHO WENT FOR GOLD (from page 54)

1. **What condition was Tanni born with that meant she had to use a wheelchair since she was as a child?**
A. Tanni was born with a condition known as spina bifida which affects her spine and has meant she has had to use a wheelchair since she was a child.

2. **What is her real name and how did she get the name 'Tanni'?**
A. Her real name is Carys but when her sister Sian saw her as a baby she said she was 'tiny'. When she said it, it sounded like Tanni. The new name Tanni just stuck.

3. **Why might road racing be described as 'exciting but dangerous'?**
A. Road racing can be described as 'exciting but dangerous' because on some downhill stretches wheelchair racers can reach speeds of 40 or 50 miles an hour - which is exciting, but dangerous because they could crash.

ACKNOWLEDGEMENTS

Many thanks to Les George, of Burry Port, who shared his collection of Amelia Earhart memorabilia with me; Steve Levers; Dr Jen Llywelyn; Jean Brewer; Evan Lewis; Caoimhe Lewis; Mary Sharkey and Colm Sharkey. Special thanks also to Tracy Edwards for her generous help with her story and photographs, and to her agent, Jo Thurley.

Annie Brewer's memory was kept alive by her great-nephew, Ian Brewer, who the author was honoured to work with on a television programme about Annie. This book is dedicated to Ian's memory.

Picture Credits:
Cover artwork: The front cover image is by Severino Baraldi. Copyright Look and Learn.
Page 2, LSE Library/Public Domain from Flickr Commons.
Page 4, Stamp (Shutterstock.com); Margaret Haig Thomas, also page 19 (AV Morgan/Wiki Commons); Annie Brewer and colleagues (Ian Brewer); Tracy Edwards (Tracy Edwards); Amelia Earhart (Les George); Tanni Grey-Thompson, also pages 47 and 53 (Steve Vas/Featureflash/Shutterstock.com); Amelia, bottom of page and also page 32 (Smithsonian National Portrait Gallery/Look and Learn).
Pages 6 to 15, All Author's Collection and Ian Brewer, except the map on page 6 (Internet Archive Book Images, Flickr Commons).
Page 17, Artwork (Dotidrop/ Shutterstock.com); Stamp (Shutterstock.com); Poster (Schlesinger Library/ Flickr Commons).

Page 18 – 19, Houses of Parliament (Library of Congress/Look and Learn); Emmeline Pankhurst (Library of Congress); Newport WSPU; the Risca Road postbox which Margaret attacked (Author's Collection).

Page 20 – 21, David Lloyd George (The New York Public Library/Look and Learn); Lusitania (Library of Congress/Look and Learn); inside the House of Lords (Rijksmuseum/Look and Learn); Margaret Haig Thomas/Lady Rhondda (Soloman Joseph Solomon).

Page 22, Elizabeth Andrews; Megan Lloyd George, 1929; Megan with her father David Lloyd George (The National Archives).

Page 26, Amelia on plane and in cockpit (SDASM Archives/ Flickr Commons); Amelia in front of the plane (Nationaal Archief, Netherlands/ Flickr Commons).

Page 27 – 29 and 35, Les George; page 30 Author's Collection.

Page 37 – 40 and 44, Tracy Edwards; page 43, Shutterstock.com.

Page 46, PA Images/Alamy Stock Photo

Page 48, Tanni Grey-Thompson (Shutterstock.com).

Page 51, Author's Collection.

Page 52, Kwekubo/ Wikimedia Commons.

Page 56, Shutterstock.com.

More from Magic Rat Books:

HEROES OF THE SOUTH POLE
Courage and Endurance in the Frozen Lands
of the Antarctic

FIGHTING FOR FAIRNESS
Righting Wrongs and Battling Prejudice

ON THE RUN BEHIND ENEMY LINES
A Story of Heroism, Action and Adventure

OVER EVEREST IN A BALLOON –
AND OTHER ADVENTURES
The dare-devil life of a modern explorer

MAGIC RAT
BOOKS

MAGIC RAT
B O O K S

ISBN 978-1-8384229-5-0

Magic Rat Books
magic.rat.books@gmail.com
www.magicrat.co.uk

Series Editor: Moira Sharkey

Designed and Typeset by Steve Levers Design, Sheffield
www.steveleversdesign.com